Celtic Mandalas

COLORING BOOK

Cari Buziak

Dover Publications
Garden City, New York

Celtic designs possess a beauty and symmetry that have made a deep, lasting impression on mankind since the early centuries A.D. The spiraled, woven, and twisting motifs in this Creative Haven coloring book are displayed in mandala form, which enhances their appeal. You'll find variations of trinity knots, love knots, and quaternary knots, along with completely unique creations. Look carefully and you'll see that many of the patterns have no beginning and no end—an impressive design feature!

Illustrations are printed on one side only, allowing you to experiment with different media, while the perforated pages make displaying your finished work easy.

Bibliographical Note

Celtic Mandalas Coloring Book is a new work, first published by Dover Publications in 2017.

International Standard Book Number

ISBN-13: 978-0-486-81423-0
ISBN-10: 0-486-81423-8

Manufactured in the United States of America
81423809   2021
www.doverpublications.com